Cultural Traditions in
Vietnam

Julia Labrie

Crabtree Publishing Company
www.crabtreebooks.com

![Crabtree Publishing Company logo]

Crabtree Publishing Company
www.crabtreebooks.com

Author: Julia Labrie

Publishing plan research and development:
Reagan Miller

Editorial director: Kathy Middleton

Editor: Ellen Rodger

Proofreader: Wendy Scavuzzo

Photo research: Abigail Smith

Designer: Abigail Smith

Production coordinator and prepress technician:
Abigail Smith

Print coordinator: Margaret Amy Salter

Cover: Vietnamese landscape painting (top, background); terraced rice fields (middle left); A women in a traditional woven hat (middle); A boy dressed in red celebrates New Year's (right bottom); colorful straw masks (bottom middle); a bowl of pho noodle soup (bottom left); a pink lotus flower (bottom left)

Title page: Buddhists pray at a religious festival in Ho-Chi-Minh City.

Photographs:
Alamy: Hong Hanh Mac Thi, p22 (inset); Danita Delimont, p24
Shutterstock: © Thoai, title page; © Pierre Jean Durieu, front cover (woman); ©, Xıta, front cover (bottom middle); © Jimmy Tran, p7; © Xita, p8; © Anton_Ivanov, pp9 (top), 22 (bottom); © Kevin Hellon, p10 (bottom left); © Duong Hoang Dinh, p11; © Tony Duy, p15 (bottom); © Tuomas Lehtinen, p15 (inset); © thi, pp16, 17; © Hanoi Photography, pp19, 23 (bottom left), 28 (bottom); © Efired, p21; ©; © Tran Ngoc Dung, p23 (top); © TonyNg, p23 (bottom bkgd); © Elena Ermakova, p25 (bottom inset); © Tony albelton, pp26–27 (bottom), 29; © jorisvo p26 (inset); © Tonkinphotography, p30
Wikimedia Commons: Thang Nguyen, p9 (bottom); © Joel Whalton, p31

All other images by Shutterstock

Library and Archives Canada Cataloguing in Publication

Labrie, Julia, author
    Cultural traditions in Vietnam / Julia Labrie.

(Cultural traditions in my world)
Includes index.
Issued in print and electronic formats.
ISBN 978-0-7787-8101-1 (hardcover).--
ISBN 978-0-7787-8109-7 (softcover).--
ISBN 978-1-4271-1956-8 (HTML)

    1. Holidays--Vietnam--Juvenile literature. 2. Festivals--Vietnam--Juvenile literature. 3. Vietnam--Social life and customs--Juvenile literature.
I. Title. II. Series: Cultural traditions in my world

GT4878.5.A2L23 2017   j394.269597   C2017-903536-3
                                            C2017-903537-1

Library of Congress Cataloging-in-Publication Data

Names: Labrie, Julia, author.
Title: Cultural traditions in Vietnam / Julia Labrie.
Description: New York, New York : Crabtree Publishing, 2018.
Series: Cultural traditions in my world | Includes index. |
    Audience: Age 5-8. | Audience: Grade K to 3.
Identifiers: LCCN 2017024410 (print) | LCCN 2017027912 (ebook) |
    ISBN 9781427119568 (Electronic HTML) |
    ISBN 9780778781011 (reinforced library binding) |
    ISBN 9780778781097 (pbk.)
Subjects: LCSH: Festivals--Vietnam--Juvenile literature. | Vietnam--Social
    life and customs--Juvenile literature.
Classification: LCC GT4878.5.A2 (ebook) | LCC GT4878.5.A2 L34 2018 (print)
    | DDC 394.269597--dc23
LC record available at https://lccn.loc.gov/2017024410

Crabtree Publishing Company
www.crabtreebooks.com   1-800-387-7650

Printed in Canada/082017/EF20170629

Published in Canada
Crabtree Publishing
616 Welland Ave.
St. Catharines, ON
L2M 5V6

Published in the United States
Crabtree Publishing
PMB 59051
350 Fifth Avenue, 59th Floor
New York, New York 10118

Published in the United Kingdom
Crabtree Publishing
Maritime House
Basin Road North, Hove
BN41 1WR

Published in Australia
Crabtree Publishing
3 Charles Street
Coburg North
VIC 3058

Contents

Welcome to Vietnam

Vietnam is a country in Southeast Asia, located on a **peninsula**. People began living in Vietnam more than 4,000 years ago when the Lac peoples arrived there from China. Over its long history, Vietnam's **culture** has been greatly influenced by China and France.

The capital city of Vietnam is Hanoi. More than 7.5 million people live there.

Vietnam's population is more than 92 million people. The largest **ethnic** group in Vietnam is the "Kinh" people, but there are many other ethnic groups such as Hoa, Khmer, and Tay. Nearly half the population in Vietnam is **Buddhist**.

The first Vietnamese people settled at the Red River Delta, below.

Did You Know?
Vietnam has more than 54 different ethnic groups.

Lunar Calendar Celebrations

For everyday life and many national holidays, the Vietnamese use the Gregorian calendar, which is the calendar used in North America. However, in Vietnamese culture, festivals follow the lunar calendar. In a lunar year, the months are counted based on the **cycles** of the Moon.

A lunar calendar uses one cycle of the Moon to make one month. The most important days are the full moon and the new moon, on the 14th or 15th day of the month.

new moon

full moon

Festivals following the lunar calendar can happen on different days each year, because they depend on the Moon cycles. Festivals are a time for families and communities to celebrate Vietnamese **traditions**, culture, and religion.

Many of the festivals happen in the spring, when the winter is over, or in the fall, when farmers have less field work and more free time.

Family Gatherings

Family is an important part of Vietnamese culture. In Vietnam, festivals are a time to gather with family and celebrate together. People often travel long distances to come back home to their families at festival time. Sometimes, three or four **generations** can live in the same house.

Did You Know?
Vietnamese people will ask their **ancestors** for advice on many important life decisions, such as starting a new business or getting married.

The father is the head of the Vietnamese family, and older children are expected to take care of their younger siblings. Ancestors are also an important part of the family, and they are worshiped at family **altars**. Family altars are an important part of Vietnamese festivals.

Families worship ancestors at family altars on special events, and on the first and fifteenth days of each lunar month.

Celebrating Weddings

In Vietnam, the road to marriage begins with an engagement ceremony, called *le an hoi*. A tray of gifts is delivered to the bride's house and marriage is proposed. To bring good luck, respected members of each family who are young and unmarried deliver and receive these gifts on behalf of the bride and groom.

On her wedding day, a bride wears the traditional red Vietnamese wedding dress, called *ao dai*. The groom also wears traditional clothing.

The bride and groom always start or end the ceremony, called *le cuoi*, by asking ancestors for their blessing at the bride's family altar. The day ends with a banquet with traditional food such as roasted pig, seafood, and many cakes. Gifts are then given to the newly married couple.

Candles represent the joining of the bride and groom. They may also be held when praying to ancestors.

Vietnamese New Year

Tet Nguyen Dan or Tet, is the Vietnamese New Year. It is the biggest celebration of the year and falls in late January or early February. The celebration can last up to ten days because of all the cooking and cleaning that is done before. Traditional food includes a rice cake called *banh chung*, and *mut Tet*, a snack of candied fruits called *mut*.

Banh chung is made of sticky rice, pork, and green beans, all neatly wrapped inside the leaves of a banana or dong plant.

On Tet morning, families dress in new clothes and children are given red envelopes of money for good luck. Families will choose a respected person to be the first visitor at their home in the New Year. Vietnamese people believe that this visit can bring good luck throughout the year.

Did You Know?
Everyone celebrates their birthday at Tet. This means that no matter what time of the year a baby is born, they will turn 1 year old at Tet.

Perfume Pagoda Festival

Perfume Pagoda, or Huong Pagoda, is the site of the largest Buddhist festival in northern Vietnam. The Perfume Pagoda festival takes place in February or March, after Tet is over. People make a **pilgrimage** to Perfume Pagoda to worship Buddha.

The Perfume Pagoda site includes many temples built right into the limestone of Huong Tich Mountains.

The Vietnamese believe that traveling to Perfume Pagoda brings good health, luck, and happiness. There are also boat cruises along Yen Stream, shown below. People often hike the paths up Huong Tich Mountains. They may also explore the caves in Huong Tich Mountains.

When visitors explore the caves, they light **incense** along the way to show respect to Buddha.

Hung Kings Temple Festival

The Hung Kings festival honors the lives of the Hung Kings. They were the first emperors of Vietnam. It is held around April, during the 3rd lunar month. People gather at the Hung Temple and set out on a pilgrimage to the top of Nghia Linh mountain.

Did You Know?
Red is the color of happiness and celebrations in Vietnamese culture. Yellow represents wealth.

Pilgrims stop at temples to worship along the journey. At the top of the mountain, there are feasts and ceremonies with a traditional kind of singing called *Xoan*. Xoan pays tribute to the Hung Kings. Sticky rice cakes called *banh giay* are a favorite food served at the Hung Kings Temple Festival.

Children of the Hmong ethnic group wear traditional clothing and perform a dance to worship the Hung Kings.

Thay Pagoda Festival

Around mid-April, there is a week-long festival at Thay Pagoda, a Buddhist temple. People burn incense and candles in memory of Tu Dao Hanh. He was a Buddhist **monk** who lived almost 1,000 years ago. He treated peoples' diseases and was also the inventor of many Vietnamese games!

Did You Know?
The Thay Pagoda is one of Vietnam's oldest Buddhist temples. It is around 1,000 years old.

A highlight of this festival is the water puppet shows, said to be invented by Tu Dao Hanh. In these shows, the water becomes a stage, reflecting the light of the setting sun. A puppeteer stands in waist-deep water and controls the puppet with a pole and string.

Puppeteers are hidden behind a screen. They make the puppets appear as though they are dancing on water.

Water puppet shows are a delight for Vietnamese children.

Reunification Day

April 30 is an important day in Vietnam's history. It celebrates the end of the **Vietnam War**, when North Vietnam and South Vietnam became unified as one country. For more than 20 years, these two areas were separate countries. April 30 is a patriotic day. Everyone gets a holiday from work and school to celebrate.

Did You Know?
The red flag of Vietnam was first used in North Vietnam in 1945. It became the flag of Vietnam in 1979.

Leading up to the holiday, there are also art and singing competitions that celebrate Vietnam as a united country. People watch television specials and do a lot of decorating, especially displaying the Vietnamese flag outside their homes.

Did You Know?
People play and perform music that was popular during the Vietnam War on Reunification Day. It is a way to remember that time.

On Reunification Day, people attend parades where there are floats, marching bands, and live music concerts.

Buddha's Birthday

Le Phat Dan, or Buddha's Birthday, happens around May. It celebrates the life of Siddhartha Gautama, the founder of Buddhism. He became known as Buddha. Le Phat Dan is a time when people celebrate Buddha's life of good deeds and behavior by doing good deeds for one another.

Buddhists line up to give blessings and gifts to monks during Le Phat Dan. This is a way to show their thankfulness.

Did You Know?
The title Buddha means "The One Who Knows."

In some cities, people watch monks in parades. The parades sometimes include floats decorated with flowers.

During Le Phat Dan, there are beautiful decorations and lanterns that hang outside pagodas, shown below. Before the festival, all the statues of Buddha in the temples must be washed. Buddhists travel home to gather at temples with their families. They worship Buddha all day and sometimes at night.

Remembering the Dead

Thanh Minh, or Holiday of the Dead, happens in the spring, on the 3rd day of the 3rd lunar month. People clean the grave sites of their ancestors and deceased relatives. They also offer incense, food, and flowers. People eat *banh chay*, shown above, a rice flour cake stuffed with sweetened green bean paste.

Cleaning grave sites of ancestors and relatives is a sign of respect.

Trung Nguyen is another festival that remembers and honors the dead. It means Wandering Souls Day and it is held on the 15th day of the 7th lunar month, around August. Vietnamese people make food offerings to the wandering souls of the dead. Afterward, the food is given to children and poor people. People also clean the graves of the forgotten dead on this day.

Did You Know?
The date of Trung Nguyen is shared with the Vu Lan holiday that honors ancestors, parents, and especially mothers. People go to temples, light candles, or give gifts to their parents.

National Day

Every year on September 2, people in Vietnam gather to celebrate the events that happened on that day in 1945. National Day, or Independence Day celebrates when the **Proclamation** of Independence was read in a public square. It declared that Vietnam was free from the control of France.

Did You Know?
Ho Chi Minh was the leader of North Vietnam after it became a free country. He is nicknamed "Uncle Ho."

Today, National Day is a time to celebrate freedom, and Vietnamese culture. There are fireworks, marches on the street, and everyone gets the day off work and school. People gather at Ba Dinh Square (below) in Hanoi, to hear the Declaration of Independence being read aloud again.

Girls dressed in traditional, colorful clothing march in a National Day parade in Hanoi.

Mid-Autumn Festival

The Mid-Autumn Festival, or Tet Trung Thu, is a fun day for children to march through the streets wearing colorful masks. The masks have faces of characters from favorite stories, legends, and cartoons.

Children may also carry star-shaped lanterns, like this one.

In Hanoi, a lion dance is performed during this Mid-Autumn Festival parade.

An important tradition of Mid-Autumn Festival is eating Banh Trung Thu, which means Mid-Autumn Cakes. Children are given boxes of these special treats to celebrate the full moon of Tet Trung Thu. They are filled with lotus seeds, ground beans, and orange peels, and they have a bright egg yolk in the center.

Banh Trung Thu are sometimes called Moon Cakes, because the yolk in the middle represents the Moon.

People light paper lanterns shaped to represent figures from stories and folk tales, such as this lantern shaped like a carp.

Christmas in Vietnam

Christmas is celebrated in different ways across Vietnam. Vietnamese **Christians** celebrate by attending services at major cathedrals, such as Notre Dame Cathedral in Ho Chi Minh City.

Nativity scenes are often placed outside the churches at Christmas time. Nativity scenes are scenes created with statues of the Baby Jesus, his mother Mary, father Joseph, and the Three Kings.

"Phúc thay
ai sầu khổ,
vì họ sẽ được
Thiên Chúa ủi an"
(Mt 5,5)

For many other people in Vietnam, the Christmas season is a fun time to go shopping, gather at parties, and give gifts. Christmas Eve is usually more festive than Christmas Day. At night, people crowd the streets to celebrate. They may throw confetti, enjoy Christmas decorations, and eat at restaurants.

Ho Chi Minh City is bright and festive during Christmas season.

Did You Know?
In Vietnam, children leave out their shoes at the front door on Christmas Eve in hopes that Santa Claus will leave them a gift inside.

Glossary

altar A platform used for worship

ancestors People who you are descended from

Buddhist Someone who follows the religion based on the teachings of Buddha

culture The customs, beliefs, and ways of life of a group of people

Christian Someone who follows the teachings of Jesus Christ, whom they believe to be the Son of God

cycles Regularly repeated events

ethnic Relating to a group with a common background or culture

generation People born at the same time

incense A material that produces a pleasant smell when burned

monk A man who is part of a religious community and lives away from other people

peninsula A portion of land that is surrounded by water on three sides

pilgrimage The journey of a pilgrim, usually to a sacred place

proclaimation An offical announcement

traditions A group's beliefs or customs

Vietnam War A long war (1954-1975) between South Vietnam (and its supporters, such as the United States), and North Vietnam (and its supporters, including Russia)

Index